So This is Me

So this is me...I'm a tad wacky and just shy of crazy.

And I love to create. Whether I'm painting fine art in my studio, drawing my wacky characters on location at shows, sitting at my pottery wheel on my back porch, or writing at my computer, the creative process is liberating beyond words. I am forever exploring new ways to express the energy inside me. But I feel forever blessed to have these gifts and vow to never take them for granted.

I'm 50-something years old and live mere feet from the ocean in a funky little surf town called New Smyrna Beach, Florida. Yes, I know. New Smyrna Beach has been officially declared the "Shark Bite Capital of the World," but the sand sparkles like white crystals and the water is a thousand shades of aqua blue. Waking up every morning to this glorious sight makes my heart tingle. I share that space with my husband, Al, and a goofy Labrador retriever named Lucy. I eat chocolate truffles while I paint—and

when they run out, I quit. I drink Perrier sparkling water so often I'm considering taking out stock in the company. I practice yoga, which for some strange reason I think will help compensate for my horrible diet, and I sit on the beach with my toes in the sand every chance I get.

I have five grown children and fourteen grandkids who love me as much as I adore them. I've taught them to dip their French fries in their chocolate shakes, make up any words they want to any tune they like, and to never, ever color inside the lines. (However, they all feel the need to assure their friends that they also have another set of grandparents who are "normal.")

Add the Color...
Feel the Tingle

There's nothing more satisfying than finishing a work of art. It adds excitement and joy to your life. Or to use my favorite tag line, you "Feel the Tingle."

The fact is, not everyone likes to draw, but everybody loves to color. Thus, anyone can experience the joy of participating in creating a piece of art with a coloring book. That's the genius of the medium. It's fun, interesting, and very fulfilling.

It doesn't matter how creative you are, you can learn about color and finish a masterpiece worth displaying. That's the purpose of this introduction— to teach you this skill.

If you already know this stuff, have a ball. If you don't, this information is way worth the effort. It will influence the way you color your entire world, from your home to your clothing to your food. Yes, even how you apply your makeup. And you will become a coloring book guru to boot.

So let's begin.

Color Selection Is Critical

You definitely want that "wow" factor when you're finished. So you need to know which colors do and do not complement each other. Do it right, and it will look like a Picasso.

The most essential tool in color selection is the color wheel, presented on the next page. Each color in the wheel is either PRIMARY, SECONDARY, or TERTIARY.

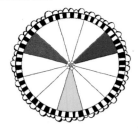

The primary colors are red, yellow, and blue. These are the root colors—they can't be created by mixing other colors. They are the pure foundation of the color wheel. All other colors are some combination of these three.

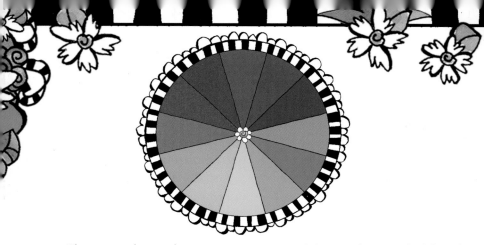

The secondary colors are orange, green, and purple. They are simply an equal mix of two primary colors (red + yellow = orange, yellow + blue = green, and blue + red = purple).

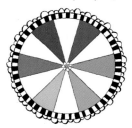

Tertiary colors are created by mixing a primary color with a secondary color. The resulting color is a matter of the percentage of the colors in the mix. There is no end to tertiary colors.

Colors are also categorized as warm or cool. Red, yellow, and orange are warm colors. Green, blue, and purple are cool colors. Selecting warm or cool colors really sets the mood of your piece. Warm colors are bold and exciting, while cool colors are more calm and peaceful.

Things really get interesting when you start playing with variations of a color. You can "tint" a color by adding white to the mix. Or you can "shade" a color by adding black.

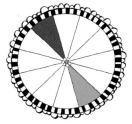

Colors opposite each other on the color wheel are called "complementary" and really pop off the page when they are used adjacent to each other. That's why you see yellow writing on purple backgrounds on billboards all over town. Or vice versa.

My Personal Twist

Since my earliest days as an artist, I have embraced the color yellow. Whether I am painting in my preferred medium of watercolors or dabbling in acrylics, pencils, markers, inks, or crayons, I almost always start with a layer of pale yellow—especially on a piece I want to be on the warm side of the color wheel. This assures that any work of art gets a wash of sunshine, whether the final colors are green, yellow, orange, or red. It really makes the colors pop. Greens get limey, oranges get a tangerine glow, reds get fiery, and yellows get even more electric.

And don't forget to leave open spaces with no color for white. It's easy to want to color every single nook and cranny with one of your fun colors, but leaving enough white is just as important to give your finished piece a lovely balance.

Celebrating the Sisterhood

...But I Like Being a *Drama Queen!*

Drama

Drama Queen (Laughter, mini), Color by Emily Maddsen
©Suzy Toronto • suzytoronto.com

Another Pair of Shoes (Laughter, mini), Color by Emily Maddsen
©Suzy Toronto • suzytoronto.com

Some days
My life
is Only
One tent
away from

a full-blown
CiRCUS

The Circus (mini), Color by Emily Maddsen
©Suzy Toronto • suzytoronto.com

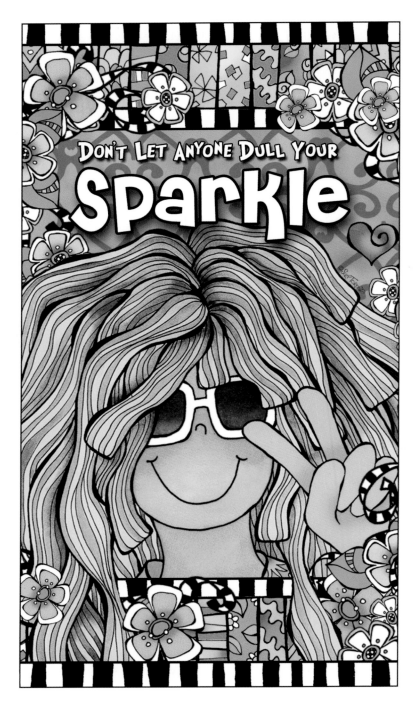

Don't Let Anyone Dull Your Sparkle (Laughter, mini), Color by Suzy Toronto
©Suzy Toronto • suzytoronto.com

When everyone zigs, it's time to zag.

Don't Let Anyone Dull Your Sparkle (Laughter, mini)

Next time your inner goofball slips out, just throw your arms in the air, let out a giggle, and give the world a cross-eyed smile.

All I want Is
Peace
☮n Earth...

(and
a really
cute pair
of shoes!)

©Suzy Toronto

Peace on Earth begins with
a bubble bath.

Becoming an Adult is the DUMBEST Thing I Ever Did

Pick a theme song and sing it regularly.

Embrace life and beam like you were born with glitter in your veins.

_____

_____

_____

_____

_____

_____

_____

_____

_____

_____

Buy the Boots (mini)

I'm a legend in my own mind.

Born with Glitter (mini)

my
best friend
has a **tail**
& a cold, wet
nose!

DOG HOUSE

©Suzy Toronto

A day without a good laugh
is truly wasted.

Cold, Wet Nose (mini)

I may appear to be a normal person,
but inside I'm completely wacky.

_____
_____
_____
_____
_____
_____
_____
_____
_____

I Do Foolish Things with Great Enthusiasm
(Laughter, mini)

Save the Earth. It's the only
planet with chocolate.

Chocolate (Laughter, mini)

When Life Becomes a
Roller Coaster,
Climb into the Front Seat,
Throw Your Arms
in the Air,
& Enjoy
the Ride!

©Suzy Toronto

When "Plan A" doesn't work, isn't it wonderful that there are 25 more letters in the alphabet?

_____
_____
_____
_____
_____
_____
_____
_____
_____
_____

Art is the signature of every
civilization that ever left its
mark on the Earth.

Art (mini)

...But I Like Being a *Drama Queen!*

Drama

Life is all about give and take.
But some issues can't
be compromised.
Stay true to yourself.

Drama Queen (Laughter, mini)

When life gets too crazy,
do something normal and
when it gets too normal,
do something wacky.

The Circus (mini)

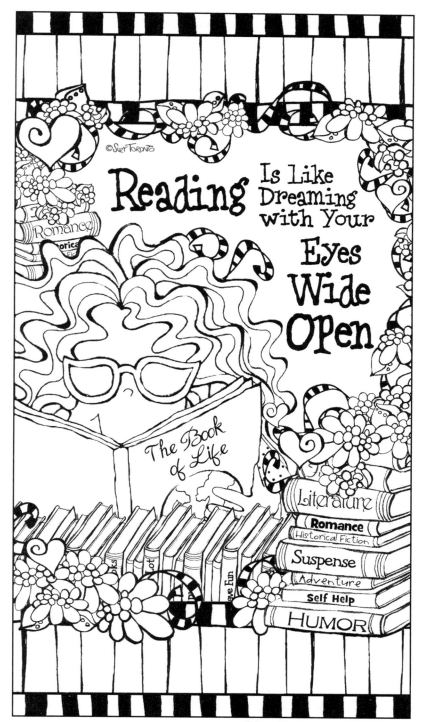

Know the rules, but learn
to transcend them.

Reading Is Like Dreaming (Laughter, mini)

Boots Don't Count When He Says You Have Too Many Shoes

Don't just give your next idea a little hop. Plunge into it with everything you've got.

Too Many Shoes (mini)

The taste of rice cakes significantly improves when dipped in hot fudge.

_____

_____

_____

_____

_____

_____

_____

_____

_____

Dip It in Chocolate (mini)

Subscribe & Today SAVE 30%

Send Me One Year at the Charter Member Subscription Rate

Annual Cover Price	Your Price
~~$39.96~~	$27.99

Canadian subscribers add $5.00, all other countries, add $10.00 (U.S. funds only). *DO Magazine* is published 4 times per year. Please allow 4-6 weeks for delivery of first issue.

Ready-to-color cardstock gift tags

YES! ✓

SEND ME
ONE YEAR
FOR ONLY
$27.99

Name: _____

Address: _____

City: _____

State/Prov.: _____

Country: _____ Zip: _____

E-mail: _____

☐ Payment enclosed ☐ Bill me later

BL15B

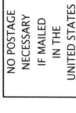

BUSINESS REPLY MAIL
FIRST-CLASS MAIL   PERMIT NO. 15   EAST PETERSBURG, PA

POSTAGE WILL BE PAID BY ADDRESSEE

DO MAGAZINE SUBSCRIPTIONS
1970 BROAD STREET
EAST PETERSBURG PA 17520-9975

As a Matter of Fact, I DO Need Another Pair of Shoes

Flip-flops make your toes feel
like they're on vacation.

_____
_____
_____
_____
_____
_____
_____
_____
_____
_____
_____

Another Pair of Shoes (Laughter, mini)

Have the faith and conviction
that you can do anything.

Big-Girl Panties (Laughter, mini)

Confront the dragons of the world and defend the weak... especially if it scares you.

_____
_____
_____
_____
_____
_____
_____
_____
_____
_____

Hissie Fit (Laughter, mini)

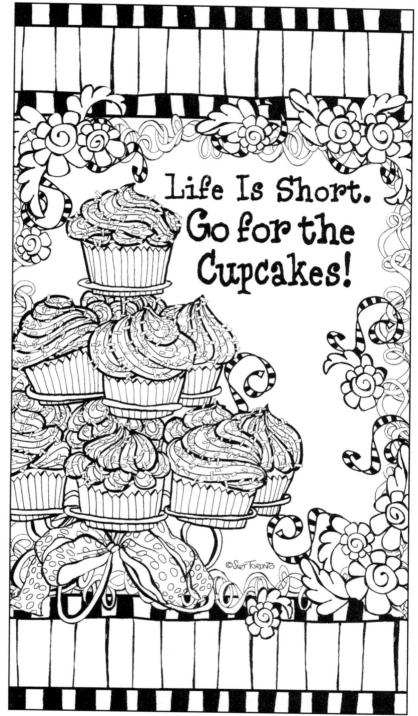

Never underestimate the power of a
cupcake to make someone smile.

_____

_____

_____

_____

_____

_____

_____

_____

_____

_____

Go for the Cupcakes! (mini)

Sometimes the threat of a can of spray adhesive and a jar of glitter held up in front of someone makes a point words cannot convey.

My best friend wears a fur coat & Purrrs

©Suzy Toronto

Some days I feel one meow short
of being the Crazy Cat Lady.

My Best Friend Purrs (mini)

An Invisible Crown: Don't leave home without it!

Put on your superhero shirt,
and be a wonder of a woman.

_____

Invisible Crown (mini)

Always Color OUTSIDE the Lines

Don't Just Break the Rules of Art... Learn How to Transcend them!

©Suzy Toronto

Life is about using the entire box
of crayons and not worrying about
keeping them all pointy.

Color Outside the Lines (Laughter, mini)

I Kiss
Better
Than
I Cook

...and I'm a
pretty good
cook!

©Suzy Toronto

Kiss like you mean it, and always be
a hug waiting to happen.

Kiss and Cook (mini)

WHEN TAKING THE ROAD LESS TRAVELED IT'S BEST TO WEAR A **ROCKIN' HOT PAIR OF BOOTS!**

©Suzy Toronto

Decide to fully live every day of
your life. The choice is yours.

Road Less Traveled (mini)

I'd Rather Be the One Who **Smiled** Than the One Who Didn't Smile Back

©Suzy Toronto

Give a smile to someone who
really needs one...then wink at them.
(It's hard for them not to smile
back when you wink!)

_____
_____
_____
_____
_____
_____
_____
_____
_____

Be the One Who Smiled (mini)

I am **Diagonally** parked in a **Parallel** universe

Where's the "pause" button when you need it?

Diagonally Parked (mini)